<u>Other books by Suzan Caroll, Ph.D</u>

Visions From Venus

Reconstructing Reality: Visions From Venus, Book 2

Seven Steps to Soul: A Poetic Journey of Spiritual Awakening

Thirty Veils of Illusion

Inner Visions Meditation CD

For more information on books by Suzan Caroll visit Multidimensions.com

What Did You Learn?

Story and Illustrations by

Suzan Caroll, Ph.D.

Multidimensional Publications

Los Angeles, California

www.multidimensions.com

Introduction

Dear Ones, I am IlliaEm, Elohim of Arcturus. I am with you today to remind you that separation is now obsolete. Hence, you are in union with ALL the multidimensional levels of your SELF. For this reason, it will take only a few moments of meditation for you to feel my Essence, as well as the Essence of the Arcturian Group Mind, within your Soul, your consciousness, your aura, your physical body, and within the physical body of Gaia.

All is ONE. Therefore, it is "time" for you to train your Desire Body for its new purpose. Desire's old purpose was to assist you in "achieving" what, where, and who you wanted. Please tell Desire that is has been re-assigned. Desire's purpose NOW is to remember—"I AM Everything, Everywhere, And Everyone for I AM "The Heart and Seed of the Crystal Matrix."

THE CRYSTAL MATRIXES

The Heart of the Crystal Matrix is in our Heart Chakra, ½ octave in frequency above our physical heart. It is the kernel of the Three Fold Flame upon which the power of our life-force burns. The Seed of the Crystal Matrix is in our Crown Chakra, ½ octave above our pineal gland in our physical brain. The seed of the Crystal Matrix is the entry point of the higher dimension into our physical earth vessel, whereas the Heart of the Crystal Matrix is where we integrate the higher vibrations into our transforming physical body.

The Crystal Matrixes are the main processing center for the "experience" to which you are choosing to calibrate. Dearest Ones, I say "calibrate," as there are myriad experiences occurring all the time and everywhere. All of these experiences are occurring in the NOW of the Flow.

When you are only resonating to the third dimension, this calibration is unconsciousness, and many of your experiences are "chosen" by the "Core Beliefs" that were activated in early youth or "past lives." You had to "work hard" to release these limitations and replace them with "less limiting" limitations.

Now there are NO limitations, as you are NO longer separate from All That Is. You are presently grounding your Soul/SELF into your third dimensional earth vessel so that you can merge your fourth and fifth dimensional Selves with your third dimensional body, as well as the physical body of Planet Earth. During this merging, your senses are being re-calibrated to the perceptual channels of the fifth dimension and beyond. This re-calibration will greatly assist you in your transformation from physical body into Light Body.

When your fifth dimensional Soul/SELF first enters your physical form, it is common to experience a great sense of "overwhelm," as your ego is not accustomed to such expanded perceptions. This sense of overwhelm can create FEAR, which, in turn, can make it difficult to stay connected to, and live from, the Soul/SELF you are downloading. It is important to remember to surrender this fear to you Soul, as what is difficult for your ego, your Soul can easily manage in Peace and Calm.

SURRENDERING FEAR

Fear to third dimensional perception is a monster of tremendous power. On the other hand, from the perception of Soul, fear is an annoying fly that must be brushed away. Do not deny your fear or try to ignore it, or that one "fly" can multiply. Brush away each moment of fear with the Hand of Soul. Fear is NOT your reality. It may even be a warning. In that case, you can acknowledge with a grateful nod, and then release the feeling of fear from your attention before it takes root in your Desire Body.

Fear once acted as a protector that warned you to be wary of certain situations. However, as you have learned, fear became a habit and infiltrated your EVERY desire and manifestation. Your Desire Body is no longer in need of fear for protection, as it is protected by your fifth dimensional Soul/SELF who resonates beyond the illusions of "need" and "danger."

THE MISSION

Once free of the need for protection from fear, your Desire Body can direct ALL its intention in one direction: THE FULFILLMENT OF YOUR MISSION. Your personal Mission is the reason for which you took embodiment in this time/space reality. There are so many of you on Earth now who have awaited this day, and you've even created petitions to show how your birth could best serve Gaia. The Service that you promised in your petition is your Mission; the Mission that YOU chose before your embodiment.

However, this is not a new Mission, as you have been working towards it, life after life, since you first "logged-on" to the 3D Game. In the last turn of the Galactic Completion, during the fall of Atlantis, Gaia had too much darkness on Her form, and nearly self-destructed. Most of you were there then to assist. During this Galactic Completion, Gaia has called in Her loyal humans who have served Her for many lifetimes. Your Mission now is likely similar to the Mission that you had then. Just as you logged-on to the 3D Game as a human, Gaia logged-on to the 3D Game as a Planet. Through your process of playing this Game with Her, you, too, have become a Planet.

Via the rules of this Game, once you are born, most of you forget your personal "puzzle piece" of the "Great Puzzle" of Planetary Ascension. However, you are now beginning to remember. You are also becoming aware that this will be your last assignment in a physical form. Once this materialization is completed, your physical body will complete its transformation into Lightbody. Most of you have volunteered to culminate this final transformation in conjunction with Gaia, as a catalyst for Planetary Ascension.

THE SEED OF LIGHTBODY

Your Lightbodies have been slowly and safely developing within the encasement of your physical shell. The casing of this "shell" which is ruled by your ego/self and is perceived as your physical body, grows thinner and thinner as the seed of your Lightbody germinates and grows within the Heart of the Crystal Matrix.

As this seed sprouts within your Crystal Matrix, it sends shoots into every cell and atom of your physical body, where the germination begins again. When each off-shoot sprouts in each cell and atom, your "junk DNA" is activated and your physical earth vessel displays symptoms of transformation. Your scientists have not found the purpose of this particular DNA because it is beyond the limitations of their beliefs; hence, the term, "junk DNA." The scientists cannot perceive what they cannot believe is possible. That is why, dear transforming ones, you must release the "concept of impossible" from your consciousness. "Impossible" is a third dimensional concept, and one that is now obsolete. ALL is possible from the insight of your Soul/SELF.

While your Soul/SELF traverses its Home vibration of the fifth dimension, it is aware of, and interlaced with, many different experiences, realities, and lifetimes that are all occurring within the same moment of the ever-present Now. Your Soul/SELF is now implanting itself within one of its many experiences, realities, and lifetimes—YOU. Consequently, you and your fifth dimensional SOUL/SELF are entering into a joint venture. You are not yet accustomed to the expansiveness of Soul's reality, while Soul Is not yet accustomed to the limitations of your reality. Nonetheless, the TEAM of human ego/self and spiritual Soul/SELF are beginning a partnership of Spirit into Matter.

THE PARTNERSHIP

Long ago, when you first entered the 3D Game, you wanted to learn how you would fare being separated from the All That Is. You wondered how it would feel to "BE" matter without a conscious connection to Spirit. Within the myriad games/lifetimes that you have played/lived, you have learned much about the separation of polarities, as once Spirit/Matter are separated, masculine/feminine, light/dark, good/bad, and love/fear are also separated.

What have you learned in your polarity games? Take a long moment of the NOW to answer that question. Ask your Soul/SELF for assistance, and please, ask us—the Arcturians—as well. At this "time," it is important to answer the question, "What Did You Learn?," for within the answer hides your Mission. When you find that answer, calibrate your Desire Body to LIVE that Mission. There is only one outcome of "living your Mission," and when it is completed—as a person, a family, a community, a state, a nation, a continent, a hemisphere, and, a PLANET—the partnership of YOU and Gaia will ascend.

During this phase of our

TRANSFORMATION

it may be wise to ask ourselves

"WHAT DID YOU LEARN?"

We have entered into "End Game" of the 3D Game.

It is during End Game that we remember the

"Rules for playing the 3D Game of Separation and Limitation"

It would have been much easier had we known the rules all along, but the

SECRET RULE *is:*

> *When you remember All the rules, the Game ends.*

In preparation for that time, let us look at the rules that we have learned so far. We have learned that:

RULE NUMBER ONE:

> The more we know,
>
> > the more we know we don't know.

We have also learned that:

RULE NUMBER TWO:

> Love has more power than fear.

Unfortunately, we also learned that:

RULE NUMBER THREE:

> Love is the first thing we forget when we become afraid.

Fortunatly, we have remembered

RULE NUMBER FOUR:

> We are multi-dimensioal beings.

Let us begin with RULE NUMBER ONE:
The more we know, the more we don't know

In other words, a little bit of knowledge makes life easier.
whereas, a lot of knowledge makes life more difficult,
as it no longer fits neatly into 3D boxes.

When we REMEMBER our SELF,

ALL we can do is step outside
the lines.
                            When life becomes too
                            limiting, ALL we can do
                            is ignore our limitations.

            When we ignore our limitations,
            WE break the rules of consensus reality
            and blur into another reality.

            However, in order to have the courage to
            "go outside the lines," we must remember

            RULE NUMBER TWO:
            Love has more power than fear.

Love reaches up to create more love,

But then RULE NUMBER THREE kicks in,
(Love is the first thing we forget when we
become afraid) and we ask,
"Is it safe to reach for LOVE?"

Then, Fear reaches down to gather more Fear.

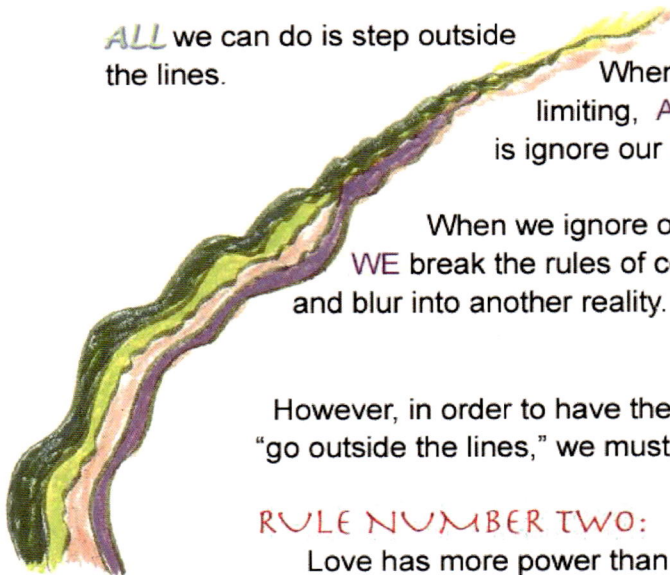

Can the delicate flower of LOVE
conquer the mighty questions of Fear?

Can the delicate flower find it's roots
in our HEART
to ease all the questions
and quite the fear?

Love whispers in response.
"Go down into the MOTHER
when your heart fills up with fear.
The answers are there
for those who will hear."
Mother Earth sings upfrom our roots to remind us of

RULE NUMBER FOUR:,

WE ARE ALL MULTIDIMENSIONAL!

For every ONE is Many

and the MANY are all ONE.

HELLO
"WE ARE THE ARCTURIANS

WE ARE HERE TO REMIND OF RULE NUMBER FIVE

REALITY IS A STATE OF CONSCIOUSNESS"

"Third dimensional reality is a hologram
that is configured by your consciousness."

"Whatever "state" your consciousness is in ~
determines the reality YOU create."

"When you are bound
by the consensus beliefs of the 3D Game,
your stae of consciousness
is limited to the third dimension."

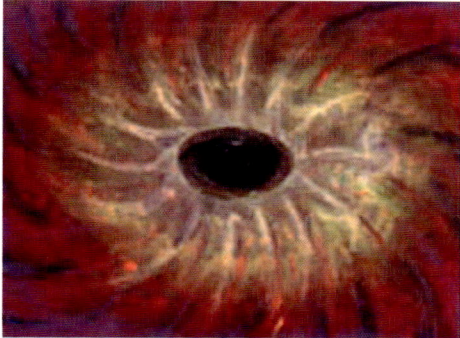

"However, if you are willing to
LISTEN TO THE SILENCE
you can break out of the 3D limitations."

The SILENCE exists in the VOID
and the VOID exists beyond... the beyond...
of the beyond... of the beyond... of the beyond..."

"The VOID is imortant, as it allows you to
'shake off' your third dimensional consciousness,
and the SILENCE of the VOID forces you to
listen to yourself."

The void acts as an ante-room. This ante-room serves as
insulation against the 'outside weather' and as a place to store
your 'protective clothing'

Once inside the VOID you can shed and store your
bulky, dense, third dimensional thought forms,
you may hear the voice ot the SILENCE whispering,

"ALL Core Beliefs of limitation

and separation are illusions."

"Go inside yourself to remember all belief is a choice.

GO INSIDE YOUR SELF
TO GO BEYOND YOUR "SELF-

To BELIEVE THAT ALL BELIEF IS A CHOICE!"

RULE NUMBER SIX:

FEAR PRECIPITATES ~ or ~ How to get a negative wish to come true.

Fear Says: "Oh, I wish _____ doesn't happen
Then _____ happens.
Voial! Fear has precipitated agaii

BUT HOW?

It was because of the Magic Box.

Fear goes in the box

and reality comes out the

other end.

BUT WHY?

Well, do you remember the ante -room?

When you go into the ante-room you step into the VOID.

Once inside the void, you drop the heavy "clothes",

of your third dimensional self

and your third dimensional thought forms.

What Did You Learn?

However, the Core Beliefs that you created as a child for protection, are the last things to go. What, or who, is such a fearsome enemy that it follows you-even into the VOID?

But, how did FEAR gain such power, and how did we get so attracted to it? Fear has always been our first protection against the angry waters of emotion. Fear is what taught us to build a mountian, an impenetrable fortress, above the waters of emotion, so that we could SURVIVE, and so that a small patch of GREEN could grow within the BLUE/GRAY of FEAR.

17

FEAR was necessary for, as we learned far too young,

    those who did not build a protective, mountian fortress

        did NOT survive.

Most unfortunately,

    even after the SUN came out

    and all was SAFE...

FEAR waited-deep inside.

For, just when we believed that it was safe enough
to release ALL our protection,
All our Core Beliefs,

THE WATERS ROSE AGAIN!

    Then we said, I knew it."

    "I was right," we confirmed.
      "What I was ofraid of-DID happen-
        AGAIN!!"

Why is fear such an inner saboteur, and why won't it leave us alone?

OR

How we make our wishes come true, even if they are negative.

BELIEF

Creates our

EXPECTATION

That Directs

PERCEPTION

To determine the

REALITY

We experience.

EVERYTHING EXISTS-IF WE LOOK FOR IT!

Why is it easier to see what we fear to than to see what we love?

"Because if we don't look out for
what we feear, we won't survive
long enough to find what we love",
   answers our protective Core Belief.

"But what about RULE NUMBER TWO
   Love has more power than fear?"
      asks our Soul.

However, if we can't hear our soul,
      we don't hear its questions
      and we default to:

RULE NUMBER THREE
   Love is the first thing to go when we get scared.

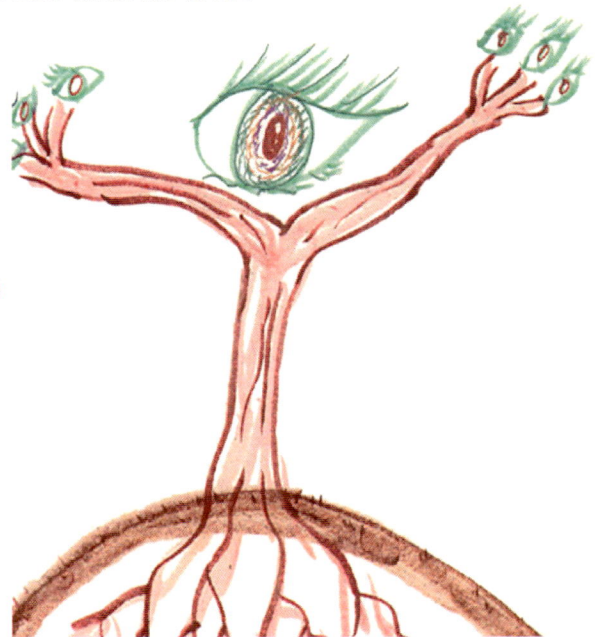

"CAN YOU HEAR US?"

"WE, THE ARCTURIANS
ARE HERE TO
HELP YOU
REMEMBER THAT
RIGHT NOW
YOU CAN
COME

HOME

(A SECRET :)

HOME IS WHERE YOU ARE GOING
AND WHERE YOU HAVE ALWAYS BEEN!"

"YOU CAN EASILY DO SO BECAUSE OF
RULE NUMBER SEVEN:
HOME IS A STATE OF CONSCIOUSNESS"

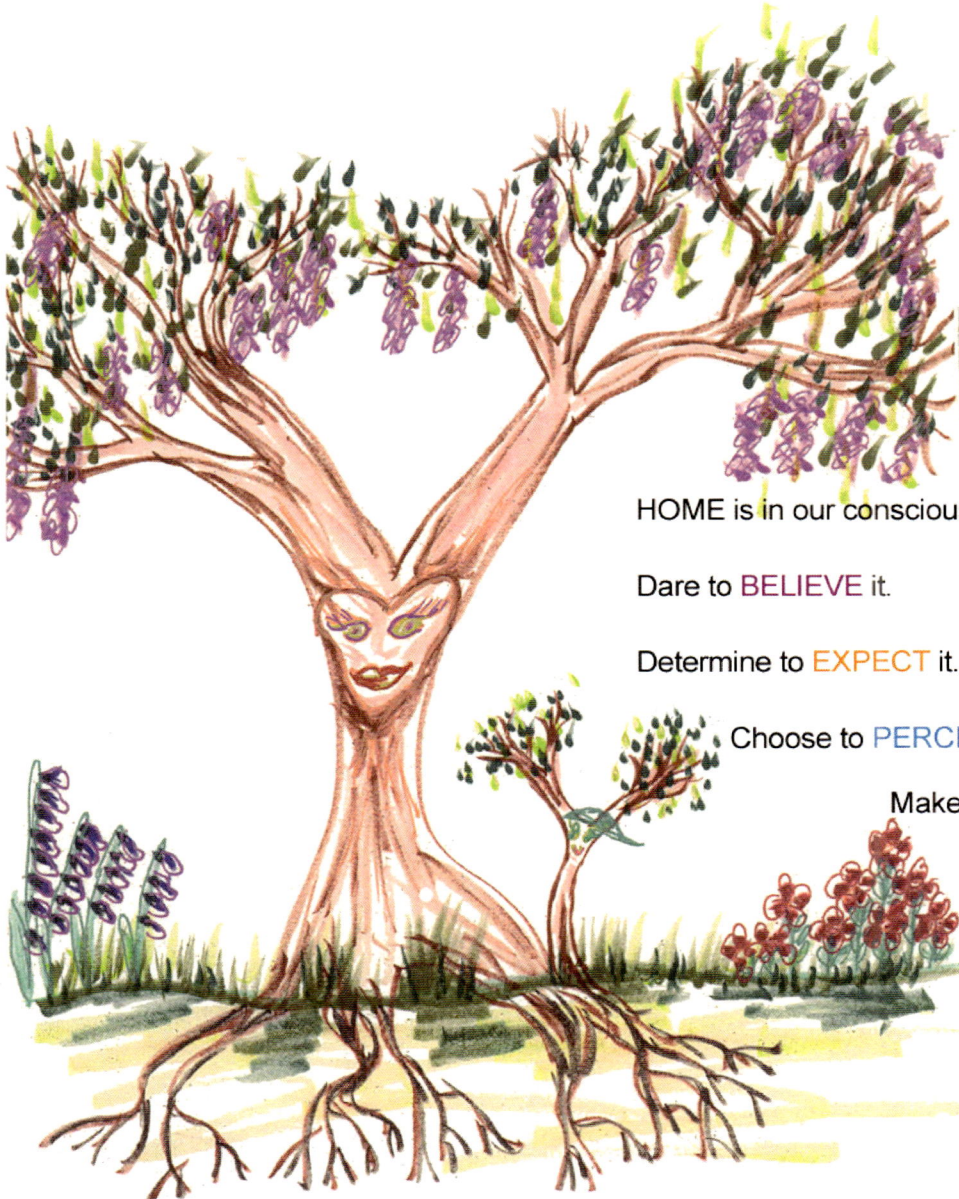

HOME is in our consciousness if we:

Dare to BELIEVE it.

Determine to EXPECT it.

Choose to PERCEIVE it.

Make it a REALITY.

RULE NUMBER EIGHT:

Love is the healing force of the universe, which leads us to:

RULE NUMBER NINE:

We can't complete ANYTHING until we HEAL it.

Therefore, since love

is the healing force of the Universe,

if we wish to complete something,

we need to HEAL it with our LOVE!

Furthermore, RULE NUMBER TEN states:

We can't get what we want "SO MUCH"

until you have learned to LOVE being without it.

LOVE SEEMS TO BE THE ALPHA AND THE OMEGA FORCE

In other words, in order to leave the OLD, we must love it free.

And, in order to bring in the NEW,

we must create space for it by LOVING BEING WITHOUT IT.

Dear Arcturians,

Please help us understand RULES NUMBER EIGHT, NINE AND TEN.

"WE ARE HERE."

"YOU SEE, IT IS ALL A CYCLE.
AS YOU GO ROUND AND ROUND THE CYCLES OF LIFE,
ALL YOUR EXPERIENCES ACT AS A "CODE"
TO HELP YOU REMEMBER.

YOU REPEAT THE SAME PATTERNS OF EXPERIENCE
~ OVER AND OVER ~
UNTIL, FINALLY, THE CODE IS ACTIVATED AND
YOU **REMEMBER!!!**"

AND WHAT DO YOU REMEMBER?

YOU REMEMBER LOVE."

"For all there is to DO,

to HAVE,

to BE,

is LOVE.

LOVE ~above all else~ will help you remember that
life in the third dimension
is just a tiny fragment of
WHO YOU

TRULY ARE!

"Remember, there is really just one lesson

with a million ways to learn it.

I AM a Multidimensional Being

Creating a third dimensional game."

RULE NUMBER ELEVEN:

If we "put our order in" to the Universe we will get

MORE than we would dare ask for!

Dear Universe, I need...

Remember to guard

against fear as it

creates as well...

RULE NUMBER TWELVE:

What we "put our order in" for will NOT come to US

before We BELIEVE that we DESERVE it.

Therefore, we must be patient--with our self!

For when the time is right

and we are ready to believe in ourself,

then the thing we dared not wish for

blooms into our life,

but only when we are ready

TO BELIEVE IN OUR SELF!

"Dear Ones,

Did you REMEMBER yet that
EVERYTHING you want is
EVERYWHERE you LOOK,
as well as
EVERYWHERE you DON'T LOOK?"

RULE NUMBER THIRTEEN:

Every time we look for what we want,
we find something we weren't looking for
and had given up wanting.

WHAT IS IT THAT WE
HAVE GIVEN UP WANTING?

Can we go into the VOID

And listen to the SILENCE

To find our ANSWER?

It is our SELF!!

Our true Multidimensional SELF

ALIVE and LIVING in our everyday life.

We have looked everywhere for SELF but in our self.

Dear Arcturians,

Is it possible to choose the reality where our multidimimensional SELF

is alive and living in our everyday life?

"PLEASE,

   CHOOSE WHICHEVER REALITY YOU WANT.

   IT IS YOUR EXPERIENCE."

But, what about the other people

   who choose different realities?

"OH, THEIR REALITY MAY "LOOK" DIFFERENT,

BUT IF YOU PROBE UNDER THE SURFACE

YOU WILL SEE THAT,

YOU ARE ALL CONNECTED

TO EACH OTHER

AND TO THE

   ONE

"CAN YOU FEEL THAT CONNECTION?
GO INTO THE VOID
LISTEN FOR THE ONE INSIDE THE SILENCE."

DO IT NOW!

SOURCE

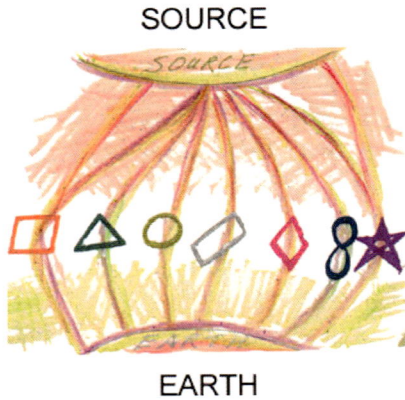

EARTH

Inside the VOID,
Inside the SILENCE

We REMEMBER

Even though every being,
creature,
and person
appears different,

THE SAME SOURCE RUNS THROUGH US ALL!

This remembrance brings us to:

RULE NUMBER FOURTEEN:

EVERYTHING comes THROUGH us not from us.

Therefore, each INDIVIDUAL

is a DIFFERENT channel for

SOURCE to express
its SELF on Earth.

Hence, RULE NUMBER FIFTEEN:

AS the SOURCE moves THROUGH us
We each create our own version of REALITY,
even if we do it unconsciously.

The question is:
WHY are there certian realities
(usually unpleasant ones)
that we create OVER
and OVER and OVER
and OVER-AGAIN?

RULE NUMBER SIXTEEN:

We know we create our reality
by combining out THOUGHTS and EMOTIONS
and FOCUSING them with our INTENTION.

But WHY do we
Have the SAME thoughts
Combined with the SAME emotions
Focused on the SAME intention

When we never really liked that reality in the first place?

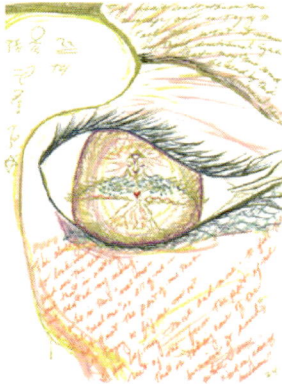

At least, we are very clever at creating each "re-do"
a LITTLE bit differently than the last time.

These "re-dos" are Life Lessons which force us to
look inside and
see our real SELF
watching our "self"
creating our reality.

These Life Lessons are a "code",
which forces our self to see,
and communicate with, our SELF.

In fact, RULE NUMBER SEVENTEEN is:
We don't have a lot of different problems.
We have only one or two problems
that affect our life in many different ways.

Prehaps our SELF, our personal channel for the SOURCE,
realizes that the 3D Game is very difficult.
Therefore, it is best to take on only a few life challenges
within one Lifetime/round of the Game.

Each life, each time we log onto the 3D Game,
 we choose one or two major 3D life challenges.

More than a few would
make the Game too difficult.

Therefore, when we enter the Game,
we "imprint" on our life challenges.

When did we choose this negative imprint to play this round of the Game?

Was it before we "logged onto" the Game-or after?
 PERHAPS IT WAS BOTH!
 Maybe we chose the parents who would make sure
 that our challenge wouldbecome evident in our Game.

Possibly, we chose parents who had the same challenges
 so that they couuold overcome them and
 show us how to overcome them as well.

How far does the apple fall from the tree?

Did we get our problems
from our parents

or did we get our parents
to remind us of our problems~
AGAIN?

Also, certain problems, or life lessons,
 have been replayed by our Soul
 over and over,
 life after life.

Each life is the same,
yet a little different,
to disguise the fact
that our life lessons
are the same,
yet a little different.

Because...

ALL only ONE in the ONENESS with many different ECHOES.

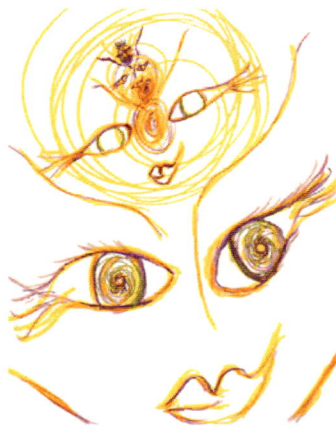

The ONENESS of our Soul/SELF, our ONE channel for the SOURCE says,

I Remember who I AM

THEREFORE, I REMEMBER MY MISSION.

Yes, we are the creator of ALL our realities,
(including the illusion that causes us to forget that fact.)

Since we are the creator ot our reality,
why would we choose to create it from the part of us
~our ego~
that specializes in illusion, and hence, cannot remember our Mission?

Would it not be better to create our reality from the part of us
~our SOUL~
that specializes in truth, therefore, REMEMBERS our Mission?

The tree needs the roots and the roots need the tree.

Can the roots and the tree work together?
Can the ILLUSION be the story and the TRUTH be the story teller?

Stories have Fear
and Love
and Adventure,
but who reads, or hears, these stories?

"WE DO, MY DEARS,

"IN FACT, WE ALL DO.
EVERYONE IN THE ONENESS ENJOYS THE STORIES YOU ALL CREATE.

YOU SEE, NOT ONLY ARE WE HERE TO TEACH YOU
THE GLORIES OF THE HIGHER WORLDS,
YOU ARE HERE TO TEACH US THE GLORIES OF ~

MADE MANIFEST!

"YOUR CREATION OF THIRD DIMENSIONAL REALITY
IS A GAME THAT THE ENTIRE UNIVERSE ENJOYS.

WE ENJOY YOUR VICTORIES
YOUR DEFEATS,
YOUR FEARS,
AND MOST OF ALL,

WE ENJOY
YOUR EXPERIENCE OF

PHYSICAL LOVE.

"HOWEVER, BELOVEDS,
THE GAME IS ENDING NOW AND IT IS ALMOST "TIME" FOR
YOUR FINAL RETURN TO YOUR TRUE SELF.

"THEREFORE, ENJOY EACH AND EVERY MOMENT
OF YOUR LIFE IN THE THIRD DIMENSION,
FOR YOU WILL SURELY MISS IT.

"NOW, IN THE FINAL ACT, YOU SHALL ALL HAVE THE SAME MISSION:

SURRENDER **ALL** CONTROL OF YOUR PHYSICAL BODY TO YOUR SOUL"

I now **SURRENDER**
ALL control of my phtsical body
to my **SOUL**!

WELCOME TO THE INNER LAND OF BLISSFUL JOY
AND
RADIANT SPLENDOR.

So that's it?

COULD IT BE THAT EASY?

All we have to do is go inside,
  through the past,
    beyond the future,
      free of fear and
        into love?
Into the love that waits inside?

The LOVE that waits inside is
the Unconditional LOVE
that our SELF
ALWAYS holds for our self.

Is it from this LOVE
  that we create an exteernal reality
    filled with LOVE?

"THE REALITY IS YOU CREATE FROM LOVE
    IS THE REALITY THAT YOU WILL LOVE LIVING:
AND THE REALITY THAT WE LOVE WATCHING.

YOU SEE, YOUR 3D EARTH GAME IS
  THE MOTION PICTURE THEATURE FOR THE ENTIRE GALAXY..
WHEN YOU REALIZE THAT FACT,
    YOU CAN LEAVE THE GAME, STEP OUT OF THE SCREEN,
      AND INTO THE AUDIENCE WITH THE REST OF YOUR SELVES.
        WHO ARE ENJOYIN YOUR CREATION."

But, how do we leave the audience?
How do we enter the audience?

"You must create a Path
    which you can follow.
This path will lead you
    beyond the drama
        through the illusion
and into the FLOW
    of TRUTH and LIGHT.

Most importantly, this path lead you INTO YOUR MISSION."

But, there are many paths along the path,
    just as there are many realities within one reality.

However, there is only ONE path
    that leads us to the ONE MISSION,
        which is the same for everyone.

To find that path, we must remember the VOID

SOURCE

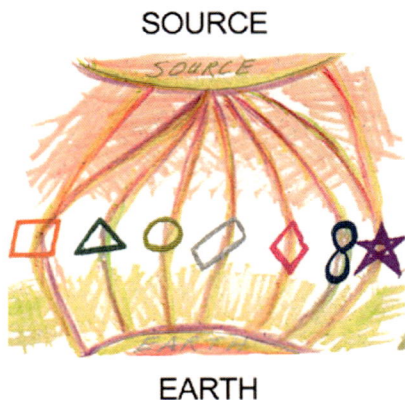

Inside the VOID,
Inside the SILENCE

We REMEMBER

Even though every being,
creature,
    and person
        appears different,

EARTH

THE SAME SOURCE RUNS THROUGH US ALL!

This remembrance brings us again to:

RULE NUMBER FOURTEEN

EVERYTHING comes THROUGH us ~ not FROM us.
Hence, each "individual's" Mission is to find, and become, the Path,
through which Sources Mission of Planetary Ascension can Flow to Earth.

"YES BELOVED,

YOUR PATH ISN'T A PLACE, OR A THING:
IT IS A FREQUENCY.

WHEN YOU ALLOW YOUR CONSCIOUSNESS
TO RESONATE TO THIS FREQUENCY,
YOUR MISSION, YOUR PERSONAL PUZZLE PIECE,
WILL AUTOMATICALLY BE ACTIVATED
AND ADDED TO THE PLANETARY PUZZLE.

"WHEN YOU SURRENDER TO YOUR FIFTH DIMENSIONAL SELF
WHILE YOU ARE STILL IN THE 3D GAME.
YOU HAVE "WON THE GAME."

IIt is then that your Soul/SELF will step out of the audience
and into YOU to give you the prize of:

UNCONDITIONAL LOVE

Once our ego/self accepts the Unconditional Love from our Soul/SELF
We can feel Unconditional Forgiveness for our human fears,
And grant Unconditional Acceptance of our human tribulations.

Remember:

RULE NUMBER EIGHT:

Love is the healing force of the Universe.
Since we can't complete ANY EXPERIENCE until we have healed it...
We must first learn to HEAL that expeerience with our LOVE!
Once we can learn to LOVE the 3D Game,
We can choose to ascend BEYOND it!

As we accept our GIFT of Unconditional Love from our SELF for our self,
our consciousness automatically resonates to the Path,
which is the frequency that ACTIVATES our MISSION.

All we need DO then, is to
FOLLOW that Path
BEYOND illusion and
INTO the Flow of t he TRUTH that:

"I AM creating PLANETARY ASCENSION."

Now, that is a reality that we would like to create
Over

And over

And over.

"IN FACT, MY ONE, YOU HAVE!

THANK YOU FOR PLAYING THE GAME

ALL MY UNCONDITIONAL LOVE
ILLIAEM